Dragons

by Lucille Recht Penner
illustrated by Peter Scott

A STEPPING STONE BOOK™

Random House 🏠 New York

To Ben
—L.R.P.

To my children Charis, Ciaran,
and Florence, who all love dragons
and suspect they may be real!
—P.S.

Text copyright © 2004 by Lucille Recht Penner.
Illustrations copyright © 2004 by Peter David Scott.
All rights reserved under International and Pan-American Copyright
Conventions. Published in the United States by Random House
Children's Books, a division of Random House, Inc., New York, and
simultaneously in Canada by Random House of Canada Limited, Toronto.

www.randomhouse.com/kids

Library of Congress Cataloging-in-Publication Data
Penner, Lucille Recht.
Dragons / by Lucille Recht Penner ; illustrated by Peter Scott. — 1st ed.
   p. cm. "A stepping stone book."
"Simultaneously published in Canada by Random House of Canada Limited,
Toronto."
SUMMARY: Relates myths about dragons from different countries, including
where they live, what they eat, and how they look, as well as how the myths
may have developed.
ISBN 0-307-26417-3 (pbk.) — ISBN 0-307-46417-2 (lib. bdg.)
1. Dragons—Juvenile literature. [1. Dragons. 2. Folklore.]
I. Scott, Peter David, ill. II. Title.
GR830.D7P46 2004
 398.24'54—dc22 2003012427

First Edition
Printed in the United States of America 10 9 8 7 6 5 4 3 2

RANDOM HOUSE and colophon are registered trademarks and A STEPPING
STONE BOOK and colophon are trademarks of Random House, Inc.

Contents

1

The Dragon Myth

A huge, scaly monster swooped down from the sky. Fire spurted from its mouth. It landed in the middle of a village.

People scrambled out of their houses. They were carrying big baskets of food. They put them down in front of the dragon and ran away. The dragon threw its head back and roared. Then it began to eat.

The village people hid in the woods. They shivered with fear. What would the dragon do when it finished its enormous meal? Would it still be hungry? Would it eat <u>them</u>? Finally the dragon lay down and fell asleep. In the morning, it flew away.

The people were safe for now. But they were still worried. What would happen when it came back?

Myths about dragons have been around for thousands of years. People once really believed that these creatures existed. They told stories about them. They wrote poems. They painted pictures and sang songs. But in all that time, nobody ever saw a dragon.

Dragons aren't real. So why did people believe in them? How could they believe in something they never saw? And how could *anyone* believe in a huge flying lizard that breathed fire?

It wasn't hard. Most people had never seen a lion, either. Or an elephant. Or a giraffe. But they had heard stories about

A Lion ·

them and they believed the stories were true. So of course they believed in dragons, too.

And people thought they had *proof* of dragons. Sometimes they found gigantic bones buried in the earth. Sometimes they found enormous teeth. Sometimes they came across giant footprints!

Today we know these were dinosaur bones and teeth and footprints. But people back then had no idea that dinosaurs had ever existed. They thought the huge bones and teeth and footprints belonged to dragons.

Is it so surprising that they believed dragons still lurked nearby?

2
Scaly and Scary

People around the world imagined dragons in different ways. The dragons in some countries were nice. Chinese dragons were gentle and kind. They brought rain so crops would grow and people would have food to eat. They used good magic to help people in trouble.

But in most countries, people thought

dragons were evil, fierce, and terrifying. Heroes had to battle them to save towns and villages from being destroyed. The dragons in these places were scary. They had enormous heads, long, snaky bodies, and tails with spikes on the end.

Most of the pictures you've probably seen are of classical dragons. Kings often had pictures of these dragons on their shields. Classical dragons were green or brown with thick, shiny scales covering their skin. The scales protected the dragon the way a suit of armor protected a knight.

Every time a classical dragon breathed, smoke and fire burst out of its mouth and nose. These fierce dragons had four legs and bat-like wings. Their tails ended in sharp, arrow-shaped stingers.

With only a sword in his hand, the Christian knight St. George faced a fierce dragon. The dragon charged. Clouds of thick smoke and bursts of fire steamed from its hideous mouth.

When the dragon reached him, St. George plunged his sword into its throat. As the horrible beast fell to the ground, a beautiful girl ran to St. George. She was the princess Sabra. The dragon had been about to eat her when St. George came to her rescue.

Sabra and St. George dragged the dragon to the king's palace. The king cried out in joy when he saw his daughter. "Thank you," he said to St. George. "You have saved my daughter and my kingdom."

To honor St. George, the king, the princess, and all their people converted to Christianity.

While many dragons lived on land,
some of them roamed the sky. Sky dragons
had large, strong wings. Most of the time
they kept them folded up. But when a sky
dragon was hunting or fighting, it quickly
unfolded its wings. *Zoom!* It soared

through the air. Sky dragons often flew
together in large groups. When a dark
shadow passed over a village and blotted
out the sun, people thought it was a flock
of sky dragons. The villagers hid in their
houses until the sun shone again.

One special sky dragon wasn't scary at all. In fact, it was supposed to bring good luck. Quetzalcoatl (ket-sal-koh-AHT-ul) was a sky dragon worshiped by the Aztec people of Mexico. Quetzalcoatl was covered with feathers. His mother was a serpent and his father was a beautiful bird.

Quetzalcoatl could change himself into a human. He disguised himself as a young man wearing a feathered cloak. Then he walked and talked with the Aztecs. No one ever suspected that he was really a dragon!

Semi-dragons looked like sky dragons, but their wings were much smaller. They hardly ever flew, because their little wings couldn't hold up their heavy bodies for long. Like classical dragons, they had thick, tough scales. But semi-dragons had a weakness. One spot on their bellies had no scales protecting it.

The German hero Siegfried (SEEG-freed) killed a semi-dragon after digging a pit outside its cave. Siegfried lay down in the pit. When the dragon walked over the pit, Siegfried stabbed it in its soft belly and killed it. Later, Siegfried tasted the dragon's blood. It gave him the power to understand the language of birds.

Not all dragons had wings. Some didn't even have legs! A serpent dragon slithered along on its belly like a huge snake. At one end of its body was a powerful tail. At the other was a fierce, crocodile-like head with a beard, long horns, and a mouthful of sharp teeth. Yikes!

All dragons—from classical dragons to semi-dragons—had huge teeth. Dragon

teeth were long and pointy. Dragons used them to tear their food apart. Sometimes they ripped heroes and kings apart, too.

A great king named Beowulf (BAY-uh-wulf) fought a fierce dragon that was murdering his people and burning their land. After a terrible battle, Beowulf killed the dragon. But Beowulf himself died a few minutes later. During the battle, the dragon had slashed Beowulf's throat with its sharp teeth.

Nobody wanted to meet a dragon—or even see one. And since dragon sightings didn't happen often, people decided it must be very hard to see a dragon clearly. They believed dragons surrounded themselves with a cloud of green smoke. The dragons puffed the smoke out through their noses and mouths when they breathed.

Picture a dragon's head, with huge teeth, a flaming mouth, and smoking nostrils. Scary, right? Now picture *two*

heads on one dragon. Some dragons even had several heads. A few had more than a hundred of them!

The Hydra, a horrible dragon with nine great heads, shrieked and roared. Hercules,

the Greek hero, had come to kill it. Hercules raised his club and smashed one of the Hydra's heads.

He jumped back in horror. The bloody head had split in two, doubling itself. Each time Hercules smashed another head, it multiplied. Soon the Hydra had too many heads to count.

Finally Hercules grabbed a flaming torch. When he smashed one of the Hydra's heads, he burned it with the torch so it couldn't multiply. After a long battle, Hercules destroyed every head. At last the many-headed Hydra was dead.

Chinese dragons had only one head.

They didn't look as scary as Western
ones. In fact, sometimes they were just
plain weird. One had the head of a camel,
the horns of a stag, the eyes of a demon,
the ears of a cow, the neck of a snake, the
belly of a clam, the scales of a carp, the
claws of an eagle, and the paws of a tiger!

3
A Dragon's Lair

In most stories, dragons lived in caves.
A cave is cold and dark and that was just
what a dragon liked. Caves are also a
good place to hide things, such as stolen
treasure. Dragons stashed away heaps of
gold and pearls in their dark homes. They
slept right in front of their treasure to
guard it.

It was not a good idea to try to steal from a dragon. If a dragon discovered a thief, it tried to tear him apart with its claws or blast him with its fiery breath.

Sky dragons didn't live in caves. They lived on mountaintops. They liked being up so high because they could watch everything that was happening down below. If a hungry sky dragon spotted animals or people, it swooped down, grabbed them, and took them back to the top of the mountain to eat.

Other dragons lived in marshes. They preferred cold, wet, misty places to caves or mountaintops. These dragons made holes in the muddy ground. They crawled inside and blew clouds of smoky mist into the air as they slept.

Female dragons came outside their lairs to lay their eggs. Most liked to lay them near rivers or streams. A dragon usually laid two or three eggs at a time.

Dragon eggs were very beautiful.
They looked like glowing pearls. Only a
fool ever touched a dragon egg. That
would have been too dangerous. It was
safer to leave them alone.

And those eggs had to be left alone for a long time. Dragon eggs took a *thousand* years to hatch! But as soon as the babies broke out of their shells, they began looking for food.

Although dragons took many years to hatch, the babies grew quickly. Before long they could roar, breathe fire, and take care of themselves. Each baby found its own lair to live in. Dragons liked to live alone.

As they grew, dragons developed terrible "weapons" to fight their enemies. Their teeth, claws, and tails were fearsome. Even their breath could be deadly!

Thor, the Norse god of thunder, raised his hammer high in the air and brought it down on the head of a shrieking dragon, the Midgard serpent. The dragon collapsed and died. But a minute later, Thor himself fell dead. He had been killed by a cloud of poison the dragon blew into the air with its last foul breath.

A dragon's breath was so terrible that it could knock birds out of the trees. Some dragons scorched everything for miles with their fiery breath. A few dragons even spread plagues and diseases. All the people who smelled their awful breath became ill and died.

Dragons used their horrible powers when they were hunting for food, fighting an enemy, or just feeling mad. And dragons were rarely in a good mood. Hardly anyone ever won a fight with a dragon. In fact, dragon spit alone could burn the hair off a person's head!

Knights often foolishly went looking

for dragons to slay. But usually people ran away and tried to hide if they heard a dragon was coming. Even though most dragons spent a lot of time in dark caves, they had very good eyesight. It wasn't easy to hide from a dragon.

Dragons could spot someone hiding behind a tree. Or crouching on the ground behind a rock. One terrible dragon could even see a honeybee flying through the air a hundred miles away!

In stories, a very brave—or stupid—thief sometimes tried to tiptoe around a sleeping dragon and grab its treasure. Bad idea. It never worked. Although some people thought dragons were deaf like snakes, they were wrong. A sleeping dragon always pounced if someone came into its cave.

The best plan with a dragon was just to stay away!

4
Hey, Dragon-Face!

The nicest dragons lived in China, Japan, and Korea. These dragons were kind and generous. They brought people luck and gave them wonderful gifts.

Many Asian dragons had a magic pearl. The pearl was usually set right into the middle of their foreheads like a third eye. A few dragons carried it under their chins. The dragon pearl cast a wonderful light. Anything it shone on grew and became more beautiful.

People in Asia thought dragons were wonderful. It was a compliment to be compared to a dragon. Would *you* like to be called Dragon-Face? In China, it was the nicest thing anyone could say about you!

Not every Asian dragon was born a dragon. Sometimes other creatures became dragons by being strong and brave.

Each spring, thousands of huge fish called carp tried to swim up a river in China. When they came to a stretch of violent rapids called the Dragon Gate, most

of them fell back. The ones who leaped
through the gate found themselves in the
middle of a terrible storm. Thunder
cracked and lightning flashed all around
them.

When the storm was over, the fish that had made it through were no longer carp. Since they had been so brave and strong, they had become dragons!

One emperor of Japan often boasted

that the Dragon King of the Sea was his ancestor. And in China, all the emperors were *called* "Dragon." The Chinese emperor sat on a dragon throne. He rode in a dragon-shaped boat. And he slept on a bed decorated with beautiful carvings of dragons.

Even the clothes that the emperor of China wore had fancy dragon designs sewn on them. These were very special dragons. Their feet had five claws. On the clothes of common people, the dragons had only four claws.

Old stories tell about Chinese emperors who got along very well with dragons.

Whenever they wanted to go somewhere, the dragons carried them on their backs. People shouted and cheered as they passed.

Chinese dragons didn't live in caves or on mountaintops or in marshes. They lived in water. Every river and lake in China had its own dragon.

A poor Chinese farmer saw a large group of dragons floating on the sea. They were spitting into the water. When they flew away, the farmer took out a boat and collected ten barrels of dragon spit. He sold them to a merchant, who used the spit to make a sweet-smelling perfume.

Some people thought dragons lived in the water to be safe from centipedes. Chinese dragons were very scared of centipedes, although nobody knew why. They were also scared of other strange things like wax, iron, and five-colored silk thread.

But the real reason dragons lived in

rivers and lakes was simple. They had
fabulous homes deep underwater—palaces
made of marble and jewels and filled with
treasure. Chinese dragons slept in their
beautiful, watery homes all winter. In
spring, they woke up and flew high into the
sky to make rain fall so crops could grow.

Every once in a while, the dragons slept so late the spring rains didn't come. Then the farmers marched along the edge of the water, shouting and beating gongs, to wake them up. When rain finally fell, everyone gave thanks to the dragons.

5
A Living Dragon

Smash! A huge, scaly creature crashes into a wild goat. It knocks the goat to the ground with its strong tail. Then it opens its enormous mouth and begins to tear the goat apart. Its teeth are like weapons. They are curved and full of tiny grooves. Each tooth is like a sharp little saw.

Is this dragon a legend from long ago?

No. This one is real. The killer is a Komodo dragon. Komodo dragons are giant lizards. They live on the island of Komodo in the Pacific Ocean. They are the largest lizards in the world. They keep growing and growing throughout their lives. Some of them grow to be ten feet long!

Komodo dragons look a little bit like

the imaginary dragons you read about in old stories. They have huge, scaly bodies, powerful claws and jaws, a long, forked tongue, and terrible breath. And a Komodo dragon's bite is poisonous. Even if the goat gets away, it will probably die from the poison.

Komodo dragons spend all day hunting. At night, they sleep in a dark cave. This real creature is very much like a dragon of fantasy.

But is there another dragon, besides the Komodo dragon, alive today? Some people think so. They think it lives in a deep lake in Scotland called Loch Ness.

People call this mysterious creature Nessie, for short. They say Nessie has a long neck, a huge body, and small front legs.

Could Nessie be a living dragon? Visitors to the lake watch and wait for Nessie, but only a few have managed to capture her on film. The most famous photograph was taken by a British doctor in 1934.

Even scientists are interested in the Loch Ness monster. In 1960, they used an underwater camera to take pictures below the surface of the lake. One picture showed a dark creature passing through the water. The picture was blurry. It was difficult to make out what the creature was.

Later, scientists used a sonar camera. Sonar can show objects underwater. The sonar showed a large creature moving in the lake!

Even trained dolphins, carrying underwater cameras, have been used to

search for Nessie. So far, no one has found proof that a dragon lives in Loch Ness, but people are still looking carefully.

So were all those people who believed in dragons hundreds of years ago right? Are dragons real? Could there be one living in a lake in Scotland?

What do *you* think?